JANUARY
2020

NATIVE POLLINATORS
Hummingbirds

Roberta Baxter

Mitchell Lane
PUBLISHERS

2001 SW 31st Avenue
Hallandale, FL 33009
www.mitchelllane.com

Copyright © 2020 by Mitchell Lane Publishers. All rights reserved. No part of this book may be reproduced without written permission from the publisher. Printed and bound in the United States of America.

First Edition, 2020.

Author: Roberta Baxter
Designer: Ed Morgan
Editor: Sharon F. Doorasamy

Names/credits:
Title: Hummingbirds / by Roberta Baxter
Description: Hallandale, FL : Mitchell Lane Publishers, [2020]

Series: Native Pollinators

Library bound ISBN: 9781680203820

eBook ISBN: 9781680203837

Photo credits: www.flaticon.com, freepik.com, shutterstock.com

Contents

Hummingbirds	4
Main Body Parts of a Hummingbird	22
Glossary	23
Further Reading	24
On the Internet	24
Index	24
About the Author	24

Hummingbirds flit around flowers. They hover in the air. Their wings make a humming sound. This is where their name comes from.

Costa's hummingbird

Hummingbirds are **pollinators**. Pollinators help plants to grow seeds and fruit.

A plant sprouts from a seed. The seed grows and **matures** and becomes a flower. The flower needs to be **pollinated** to make new seeds and fruit. How does this happen? It depends on **pollen**.

Pollen is the powder found in flowers. Nectar is found deep inside flowers too. Nectar is sweet. Hummingbirds fly from flower to flower to drink nectar. Pollen sticks to them. The hummingbirds fly to other flowers. The pollen falls off of them and onto the flowers. This is pollination.

Allen's hummingbird

Hummingbirds are native to the Americas. That makes them native pollinators.

Anna's hummingbird

13

Hummingbirds use their beaks to drink nectar. Their beak is long and narrow. Their tongue is long too. They use their tongues like straws.

Broad-billed hummingbird

15

The hummingbird is one of the smallest birds in the world. One kind is as small as a dime. Hummingbirds hover. They also fly forward, backward, and upside down.

Black-chinned hummingbird

17

Many wildflowers depend on hummingbirds for pollination. Honeysuckles and morning glories are two. Blueberry flowers need them too. Bears, birds, and people love to eat blueberries.

Alaskan blueberries

Hummingbirds are fun to watch. Flowers need them to grow.

Anna's hummingbird

21

MAIN BODY PARTS
OF A
Hummingbird

The wings of a hummingbird are different from other birds. Hummingbirds can turn their wings during flight. Make your hand go flat and then turn it up and down. That is what hummingbirds can do with their wings. This makes it possible for them to fly forwards and backwards. They can even fly sideways and upside down.

GLOSSARY

beak
The hard, curved-mouth parts of a bird

hover
To stay in the air over one spot

mature
Fully grown

native
A bird that has lived in America from the earliest times; not from another country

nectar
A sugary drink found inside flowers

pollen
A fine, yellow powder found inside flowers

pollinate
To move pollen from one flower and take it to another flower which allows that flower to turn into seeds or fruit

pollinators
Insects, birds, or animals that spread pollen from one flower to another

pollination
A process where pollen is spread

FURTHER READING

Sill, Cathryn. *About Hummingbirds: A Guide for Children.* Atlanta, GA: Peachtree Publishers, 2011.

Arnim, Aife. *A Bird Watcher's Guide to Hummingbirds.* New York: Gareth Stevens Publishing, 2018.

Bader, Bonnie. *Hummingbirds.* New York: Grosset & Dunlap, an imprint of Penguin Group, 2015.

Hirsch, Rebecca A. *Ruby-throated Hummingbirds: Tiny Hovering Birds.* Minneapolis: Lerner Publications, 2016.

Pollination (Science Readers: Content and Literacy). Teacher Created Materials, 2014.

ON THE INTERNET

https://www.youtube.com/watch?v=EkAhYmXWuFU
Here you'll find a video for children with facts about hummingbirds.

https://www.hummingbird-guide.com/hummingbirds-for-kids.html
This site has facts and activities about hummingbirds.

https://kidsgrowingstrong.org/birds/
This site talks about the importance of hummingbirds and compares bird bills.

https://www.hummingbirdcentral.com/hummingbirds-for-kids.htm
Facts about hummingbirds and some stunning pictures are featured here.

INDEX

Beak	14, 22
Blueberries	18
Honeysuckle	18
Morning glories	18
Nectar	10, 14

About the Author

Roberta Baxter lives in Colorado. She enjoys exploring in the mountains where hummingbirds are a familiar sight. She has written more than 40 nonfiction books.